NOTE TO PARENTS

Apologetics Press is a non-profit organization dedicated to the defense of New Testament Christianity. For over 30 years, we have provided faith-building materials for adults. We also have produced numerous products (*Discovery* magazine, our *Explorer Series*, children's tracts, and various books) for young people from infancy through high school. We now are pleased to present a new series of books.

The Apologetics Press Advanced Reader Series is a step up from our Early Reader Series. The Advanced Reader Series is aimed at children in 2nd-3rd grades. Although our Advanced Readers have about the same number of pages as our Early Readers, the Advanced Readers have twice as much text, as well as more advanced words.

With beautiful, full-color pictures and interesting facts about God's wonderfully designed Creation, your children will develop a greater love for reading and for their grand Designer.

We hope you enjoy using the Apologetics Press Advanced Reader Series to encourage your children to read, while at the same time helping them learn about God and His Creation.

D1445038

The Amazing Human Body, Designed by God

by Caleb Colley

© 2010 Apologetics Press, Inc.

All rights reserved. No part of this book may be reproduced in any manner whatsoever without the written permission from the publisher.

ISBN-13: 978-1-60063-022-4

Library of Congress: 2009913961

Layout and design: Rob Baker
Printed in China

APOLOGETICS PRESS, INC.
230 LANDMARK DRIVE
MONTGOMERY, AL 36117-2752

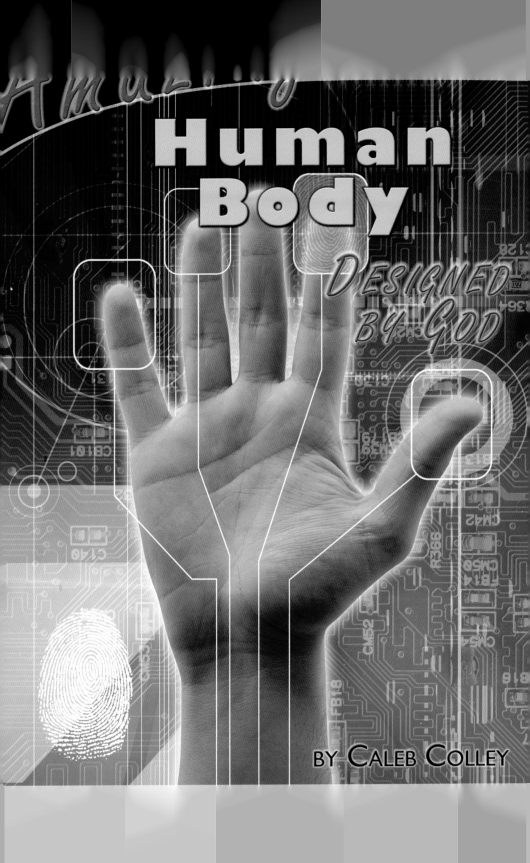

Amazing

Human
Body

Designed by God

by Caleb Colley

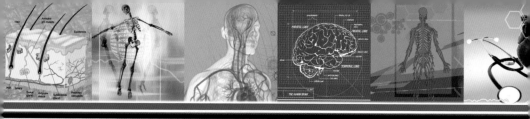

Every day, we do many different things. From the time we climb out of bed in the morning, until we go to sleep at night, our bodies are active. We sit and stand, work and relax, run and walk, and think very hard.

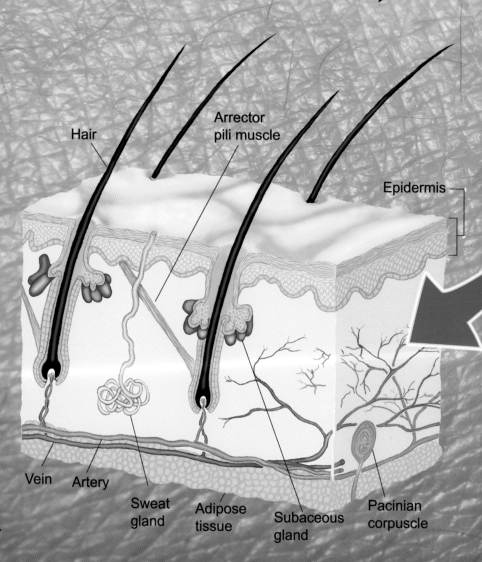

Hair

Arrector pili muscle

Epidermis

Vein   Artery

Sweat gland   Adipose tissue   Subaceous gland   Pacinian corpuscle

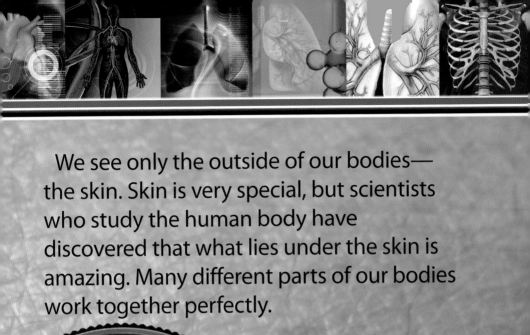

We see only the outside of our bodies—the skin. Skin is very special, but scientists who study the human body have discovered that what lies under the skin is amazing. Many different parts of our bodies work together perfectly.

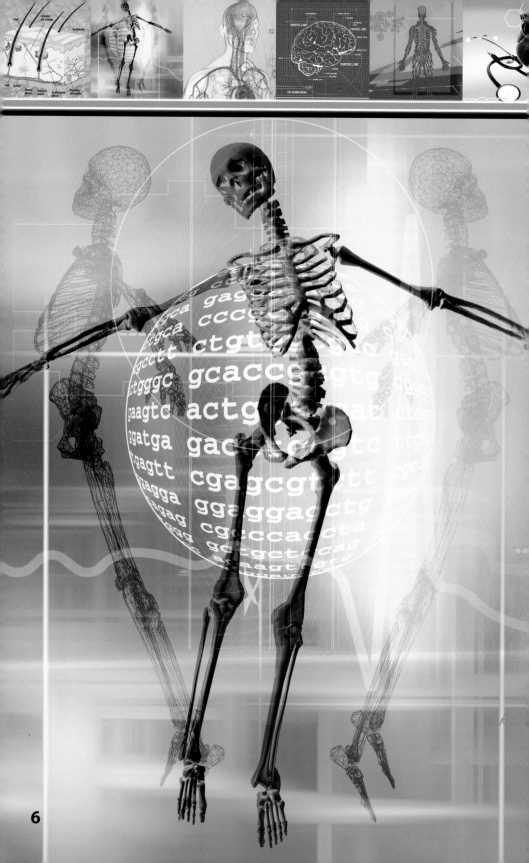

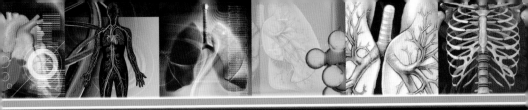

Remember what King David wrote about God: "I will praise You, for I am fearfully and wonderfully made" (Psalm 139:14). David believed that God created the human body.

This is exactly what we read in Genesis 2:7: "And the Lord God formed man of the dust of the ground, and breathed into his nostrils the breath of life; and man became a living being."

On the other hand, evolutionists do not believe that God designed everything. Evolutionists think that our bodies work right by accident. They think that, over billions of years, nature alone caused life to work correctly. According to evolution, simple kinds of life (like worms) slowly changed into very complex kinds of life. Which do you think is responsible for our bodies: God or evolution?

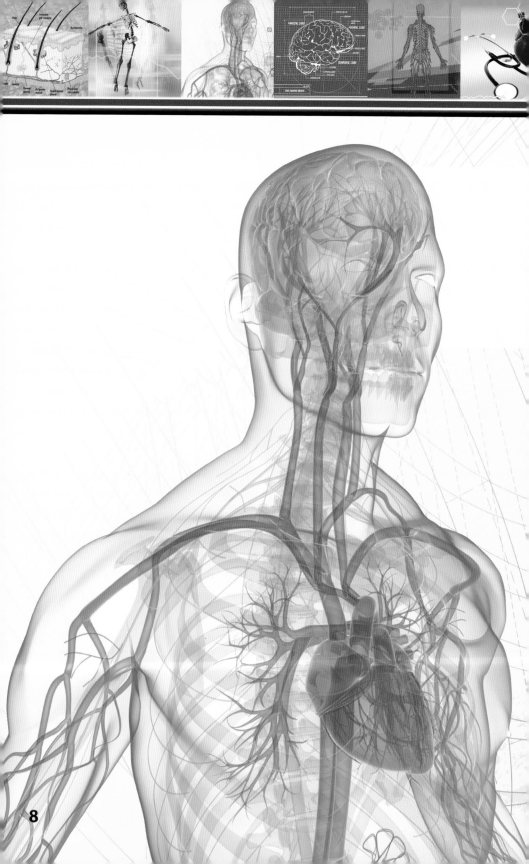

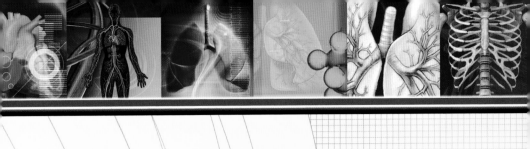

To help you answer this question, let's think about a few of the wonderful things the body can do. Your bones, ears, heart, lungs, eyes, and brain all point to the great Designer—God.

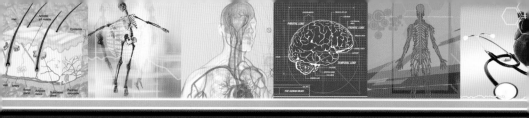

The Brain: Your Body's Command Center

The brain is like a super computer that controls how our bodies work. The brain sends messages through the spinal cord and nerve cells, to the rest of the body. The whole system of the brain and nerve cells is called the nervous system.

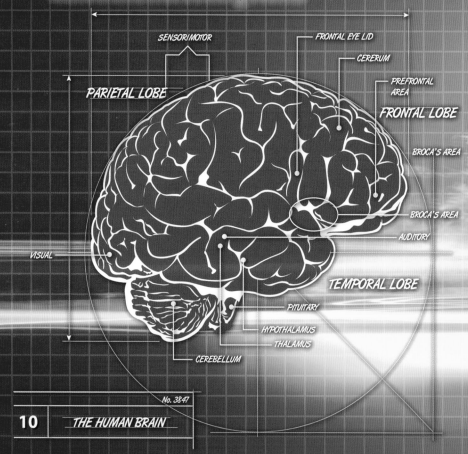

SENSORIMOTOR

FRONTAL EYE LID

CERERUM

PREFRONTAL AREA

PARIETAL LOBE

FRONTAL LOBE

BROCA'S AREA

BROCA'S AREA

AUDITORY

VISUAL

TEMPORAL LOBE

PITUITARY

HYPOTHALAMUS

THALAMUS

CEREBELLUM

No. 3847

THE HUMAN BRAIN

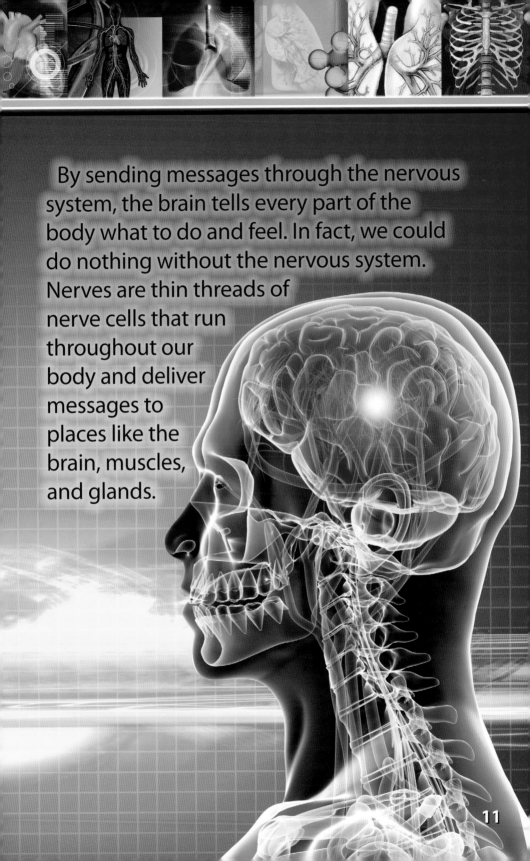

By sending messages through the nervous system, the brain tells every part of the body what to do and feel. In fact, we could do nothing without the nervous system. Nerves are thin threads of nerve cells that run throughout our body and deliver messages to places like the brain, muscles, and glands.

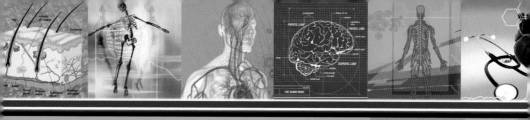

Could the nervous system have evolved? Absolutely not, for two reasons: (1) The nervous system is too complicated to be the result of an accident. Simple things do not get more complex on their own. In fact, the opposite is true. (2) It takes a cell to make a cell. However, evolutionists do not know where the first, tiny nerve cell came from. So, evolutionists cannot explain why the nervous system exists at all.

Our bodies cannot survive without a nervous system. On the other hand, the nervous system would have nothing to do if the rest of the body were not there. So which came first: the nervous system, or the rest of the body? Evolutionists have no good answer, but creationists (people who believe that God created the Universe) know that God created the first man with a complete body and nervous system.

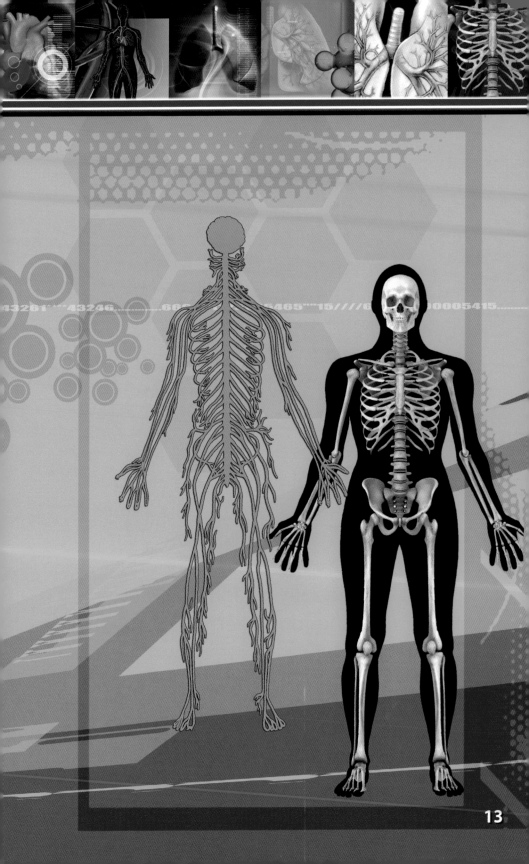

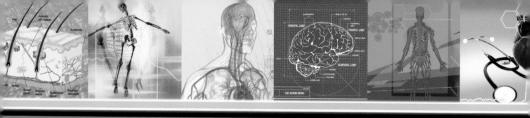

Blood Vessels: Life On the Go

God said: "The life of the flesh is in the blood" (Leviticus 17:11). Humans cannot survive without blood, because blood gives the body oxygen and other nutrients. But blood does not stay still. It has to go to all parts of the body. For this, each of us has a special pump, called the heart, and a system of tubes called blood vessels.

The heart pumps blood to every cell in the body. The blood travels through 60,000 miles of small tubes called veins and arteries. That length is more than twice the distance around the world! Blood vessels are specially designed to fit around bones and other body parts. During one year, your blood vessels transport 700,000 gallons of blood.

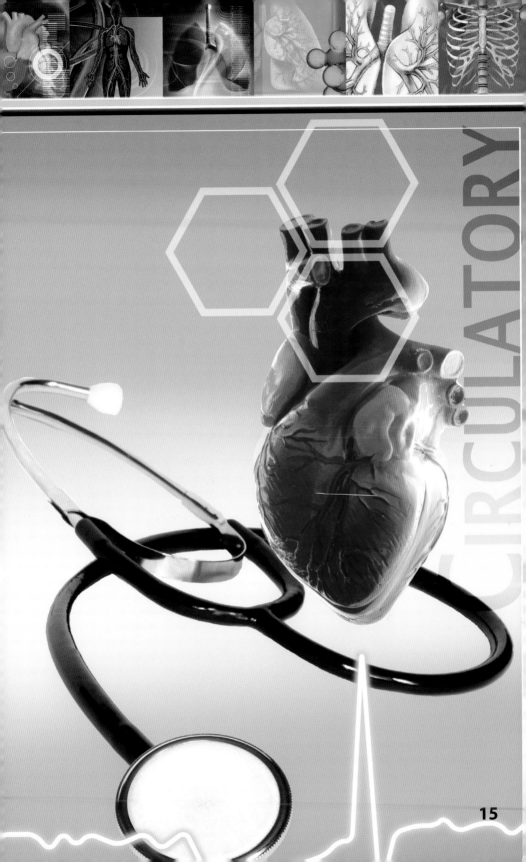

CIRCULATORY

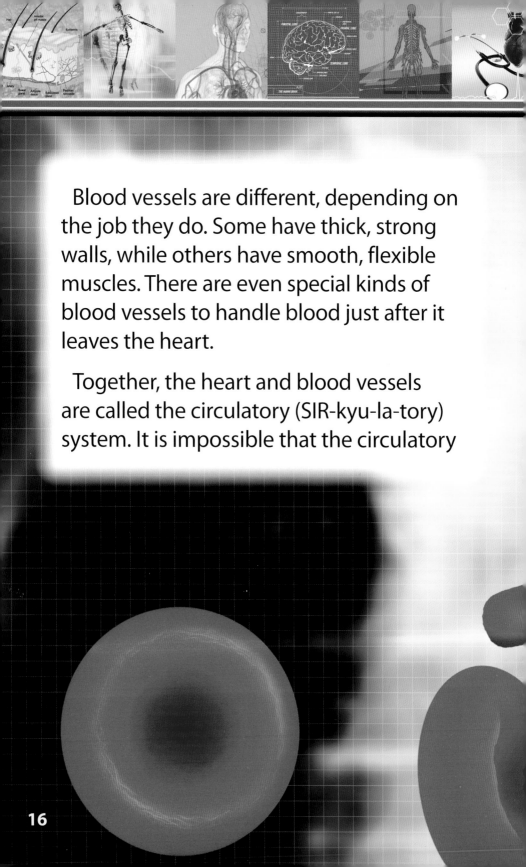

Blood vessels are different, depending on the job they do. Some have thick, strong walls, while others have smooth, flexible muscles. There are even special kinds of blood vessels to handle blood just after it leaves the heart.

Together, the heart and blood vessels are called the circulatory (SIR-kyu-la-tory) system. It is impossible that the circulatory

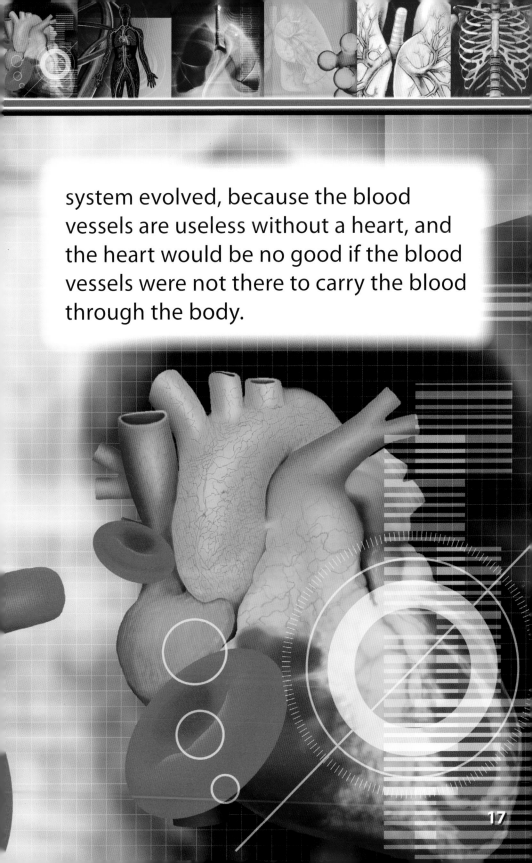

system evolved, because the blood vessels are useless without a heart, and the heart would be no good if the blood vessels were not there to carry the blood through the body.

No human being can live without blood vessels or a heart. If a man had a heart, but his blood vessels had not "evolved" yet, he could not survive. On the other hand, if a person had blood vessels, but evolution had not yet finished working on the heart, then the man would die. In either case, evolution doesn't stand a chance.

The other answer makes sense: God designed the human body with the full circulatory system in place and ready to work. When God created the first man, Adam, his heart was ready to pump the blood, and his blood vessels were ready to carry it. In fact, your heart has been pumping blood through your blood vessels since before you were born.

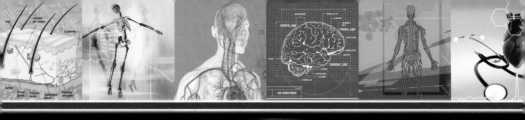

Breathing In and Out

Usually, we breathe without even thinking about it. But if you ever held your breath for more than a few seconds, then you know that the body's **respiratory system** is very important. The respiratory system gives oxygen to the blood (remember that all cells in our bodies need oxygen). Have you thought about the parts of your body that work when you breathe? You use your mouth, nose, trachea, lungs, diaphragm, and more.

Some animals take in oxygen through their skin. This process is called diffusion. Humans do not get oxygen by diffusion. Instead, we take in air through the mouth or nose. When you inhale air, your lungs get bigger to make room for the oxygen in the air you breathe. In the lungs, oxygen connects to

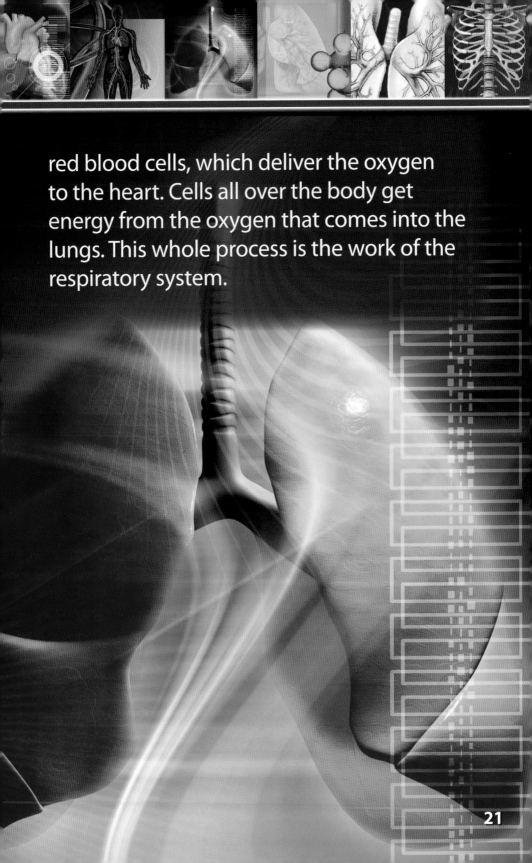

red blood cells, which deliver the oxygen to the heart. Cells all over the body get energy from the oxygen that comes into the lungs. This whole process is the work of the respiratory system.

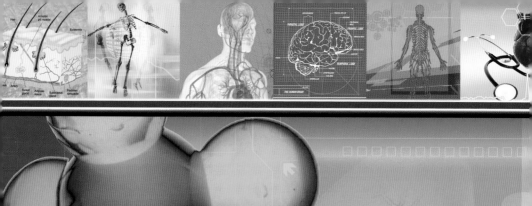

In order for the body to get the energy it needs, chemicals work throughout the respiratory system. Oxygen helps our body's chemicals to break down the food we eat, and release energy from the food to the cells.

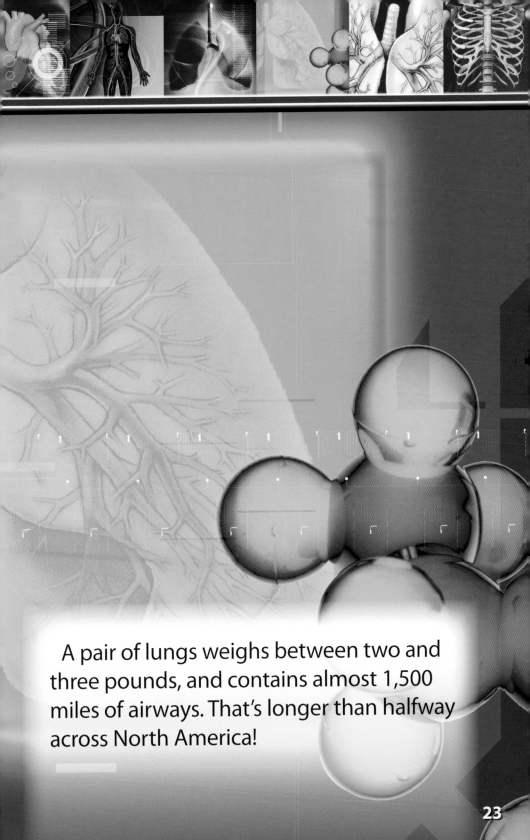

A pair of lungs weighs between two and three pounds, and contains almost 1,500 miles of airways. That's longer than halfway across North America!

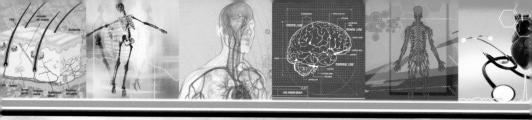

Without complete lungs and the other parts of the respiratory system, the first human being could not have survived. Also, the chemicals in the respiratory system are far too complex to have happened just right—by accident—in the first human being. The cells of that first person would have died before getting enough oxygen. Evolutionists do not have a good way to explain how the human body got here.

Creationists, on the other hand, know that God created the first human being with a complete respiratory system. God breathed into Adam the "breath of life" (Genesis 2:7).

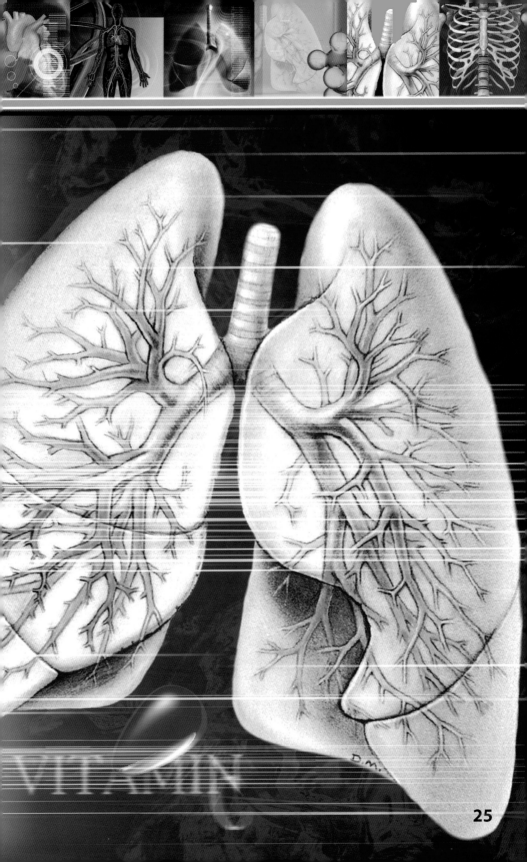

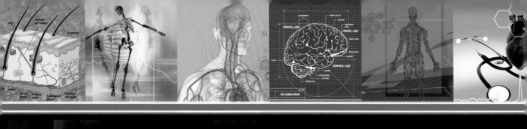

Bones: Support for Success

The human body has 206 bones, and each of them does an important job. Bones protect our body, support us when we stand up, sit up, or look up, produce blood for our bodies, store minerals, and allow us to move smoothly. Some bones, like those in your ear, are short, while some leg bones are long. The whole set of bones in the body is called the **skeletal system**.

Bones need muscles in order to help us. Muscles come in all sizes. Some, like leg muscles, are big. Others, like the muscles in your little finger, are very small. Bones and muscles depend on the circulatory and respiratory systems for energy.

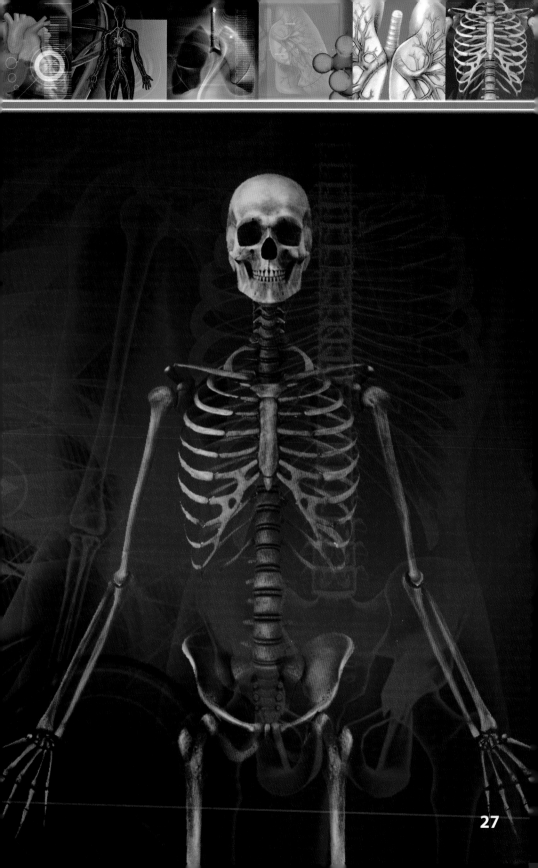

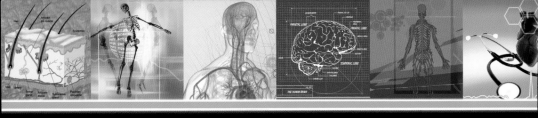

Evolutionists think that early creatures did not have bones, but that bones gradually came from hard parts of the animals' bodies. Scientists know, however, that it takes much more than just a tough body part to make a bone. In fact, without the circulatory system and the **digestive system** (which takes care of the food we eat), bones never could form. However, the other systems of the body need the skeletal system in order to work right.

The first human being would have died without a working skeletal system. It is impossible that bones evolved. Creationists know the truth: God created the first humans with perfect bones.

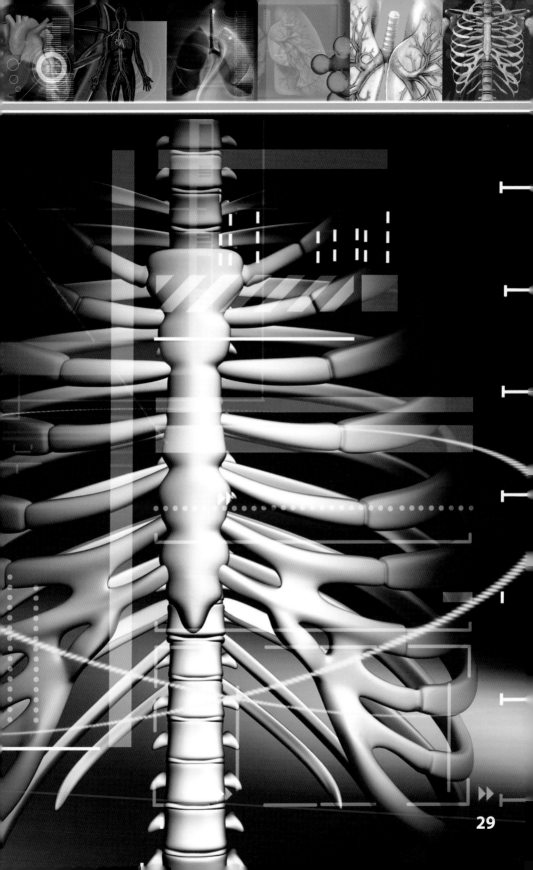

Behind Every Design, There Is a Designer

Our bodies are far more complicated than the best computers. Also, our cells contain more information than millions of books. And all the parts of our bodies—muscles, bones, veins, brain cells—work together so that we can live.

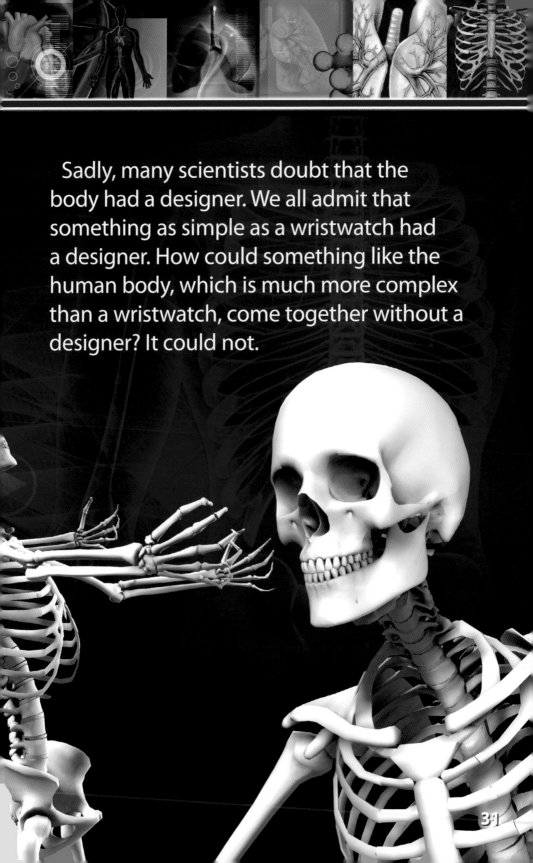

Sadly, many scientists doubt that the body had a designer. We all admit that something as simple as a wristwatch had a designer. How could something like the human body, which is much more complex than a wristwatch, come together without a designer? It could not.

God designed our bodies, and knows everything about them. The Bible says that serving God will be "health to your flesh, and strength to your bones" (Proverbs 3:8). How foolish for a person to use his body to disobey the One Who created human beings. Your body and soul will be blessed if you serve the Lord.

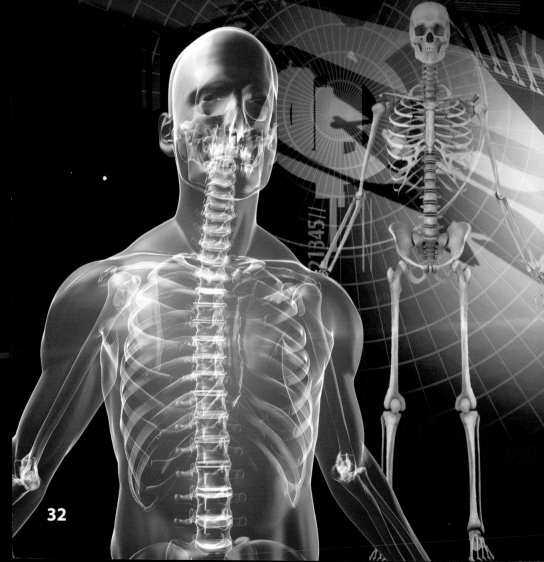